I WROTE MY DESTINY

AADYA SINGH

ISBN 979-888555621-7

TO MY MOTHER ,MY SISTER AND MY FATHER

WITHOUT YOU I WOULD NEVER BE ABLE TO

ACHIEVE ANYTHING IN THE WORLD.

Contents

Contents

Foreword

IT ISN'T MY FIRST TIME WRITING, BUT WHENEVER I START WRITING

MY HANDS START SHIVERING AND I START TO PANICK BUT THIS TIME I WON'T

BECAUSE I'M CONFIDENT THAT WHATEVER THING I'M ABOUT TO TELL YOU

ARE REALLY NOT CONFUSING.SO WHEN I WAS SMALL LIKE 5 OR 6 YEARS OLD

I USED TO BE REALLY SHY AND NOT THAT OUTSPOKEN BUT I SAW PEOPLE ,

MY FRIENDS MY TEACHERS,THEY KNEW I CAN BE A BETTER VERSION OF MYSELF

I CAN DO BETTER AND I THINK I REALLY DID,THEY CHANGED ME,CAUSE THERE IS A

SAYING THAT "PEOPLE CHANGE PEOPLE", AND IT REALLY HAPPENED,THOSE TIMES THOSE

PEOPLE TAUGHT ME THAT EVERING IS POSSIBLE IF YOU THINK YOU CAN DO IT.

A NOW I WRITE POETRY,CAUSE I KNOW I'M GOOD TELLING PEOPLE ABOUT ME AND MY

GOALS,MY LIFE AND MY VIEWS ABOUT A PARTICULAR THING IN JUST FW LINES,AND THAT

IS WHAT SPECIAL ABOUT ME.

Preface

EVERYTHING WRITTEN IN THIS BOOK HAS REALLY HAPPENED TO ME,

I WROTE A FEW OF MY POEMS AT MIDNIGHT ,I WOKE UP TOOK A PENCIL

AND STARTED WRITING WHATEVER WAS COMMING IN MY MIND AT THAT

TIME , IT WAS MAGICAL ,EVERTHING I WROTE MADE SENSE ,AND FOR ME THE

IT WAS A MAGNIFICENT NIGHT.

Acknowledgements

I'M REALLY THANKFUL TO THE PEOPLE WHO SUPPORTED ME

TO WRITE THIS BOOK,ITS A DREAM COME TRUE FOR ME .TILL NOW

I HAVE MET A LOT OF PEOPLE IN MY LIFE SOME WERE TRULY GOOD

SOME WERE NOT BUT BECAUSE OF THEM I TURNED MY ANGER, MY HAPPINESS ,

MY SADNESS INTO POEMS AND AS YOU CAN SEE WHERE I AM BECAUSE OF THEM.

Prologue

MY LIFE TOOK A TURN WHEN I STARTED WRITING , EVERYTHING BECAME A GAME

FOR ME AND WHEN MY FIRST BOOK GOT PUBLISHED IT WAS UNBELIEVABLE FOR ME

I THOUGH I WAS IN A DREAM I TOLD MY MOTHER TO PINCH ME OUCH!"I SAID BUT IT WAS REAL.

1. AS TIME PASSES BY

AS TIME PASSES BY
I THINK WHAT DO I COMPLY,
COOK OR WRITE A BOOK,
SHOULD I SPEAK
OR USE SOMEBODY
ELESE'S TECHNIQUE
TO BE AT THE PEAK,
WHEN I CAN'T THINK
I TRY TO DO VARIOUS
KIND OF THINGS,
I PAINT AND TRY
MY BEST TO CREATE
SOMETHING THAT HAS
BEEN AWAITING FOR
A LONG TIME,

2. DIFFERENT

WHAT IS DIFFERNT
THAT WE DO EVERYDAY
SOMETIMES WE ARE GALLANT
BUT HALF OF THE TIMES
WE ARE SILENT,
WE EAT,WE SLEEP,
WE BREATHE BUT THAT'S
WHAT WE DO EVERY
WEEK,
WE LAUGH , WE SMILE ,
WE TALK,WELL THAT'S SOMETHING
WE DON'T DO A LOT,
WE CLOSE OUR EYES
AND REVISE,WHAT WE HAVE
IMPROVISE,
IT WAS BETTER CAUSE IT
WAS A SURPRISE,
WHEN SOMEONE COMES
DIFFERNT IN OUR LIFE
EVERYTHING SUDDENLY
BECOMES DIVINE.

3. MAGIC

ITS IN YOU,ITS IN
ME ,ITS IN EVERYTHING
WE SEE,
YOU MAY THINK
I'M A WIZARD WHO HAS
COME FROM ANOTHER
LAND,BUT THAT'S
JUST WHO I AM,
I MAY HAVE FUNKY
HAIR AND CRAZY SMILE
BUT THAT'S WHAT
I LIKE,
I CAN FLY ,I CAN
READ YOU'R MIND SO
BE CAREFUL I CAN
MAKE YOU BLIND,
I CAN DO ANYTHING
TO MAKE YOU SCARE
AWAY,BUT IN REAL
I JUST WANT TO
MAKE YOU STAY.

4. DREAM!

SOME ARE BIG,SOME
ARE SMALL,WISH COULD
HAVE THEM ALL,
SOME DREAMS ARE SO
BIG,YOU REMEMBER
FOREVER ,BUT
OTHERS YOU
FORGET,
SOME LAST A DAY,
SOME LAST A LIFETIME,
DON'T ONLY DREAM
AT NIGHT,ALSO
IN THE MORNING,
SOME ARE POSSIBLE,SOME
ARE NOT,BUT YOU HAVE
TO DREAM MORE
THAT'S ALL YOU
HAVE GOT.

5. ABOVE THE SKY!!

I WANT TO TOUCH THE
SKY,BUT I DON'T
KNOW HOW TO FLY,
BUT I'LL BORROW
SOMEONE'S WINGS SO
I CAN TOUCH THE SKY,
I WANT TO TOUCH THE
SUN,BUT EVERY EVIL
UNDER THE SUN
THERE IS A
REMEDY OR
THERE'S A
NONE,
I WANT TO TOUCH THE
MOON, I'LL SIT IN
MY HOT AIR BALLOON
AND FLY AWAY
TO THE MOON
AS SOON,OTHERWISE
IT WILL BE
NOON,
I WANT TO TOUCH THE
MARS ,THEN I LOOK

BACK AT YOU,AND
THEN AT THE STARS, BUT ONE
DAYI WILL TOUCH
THE MARS,
I WANT TO TOUCH
THE END OF THE EARTH,
I KNOW IT'S NOT
POSSIBLE BUT STILL
KNOW IT'S ROSABEL.

6. MY WORLD!

WHEN I CLOSE MY EYES
AND WANT TO FELL SOMETHING
NICE, I ENTER INTO
MY WORLD,
NO ONE AROUND ME,
JUST ME AND MY IMPERFECT
SELF,I CAN FELL THE
BEST THING WITHOUT
EVEN TOUCHING IT,
EVEN WHEN I'M JUST
WATCHING IT,
OUTSIDE I'M FULL
OF DARKNESS,BUT ON THE
INSIDE I'M A GIRL WHO
CAN'T LIVE WITHOUT
LIGHT,
I BELIVE IN THE UNSEEN
BUT THATS NOT REALITY
IT'S JUST A THING I
IMAGINE,
I'M GOING TO TRAVEL
THE WHOLE WORLD AS SOON
AS I'M OUT OF MY

OWN WORLD.

7. THIRTEEN YEARS!

THIRTEEN YEARS BACK
I WAS ON YOUR LAP,
CRYING LIKE CRAZY,
BUT STILL LOOKING AT ME
LIKE I'M DAISIES,
WHEN I WAS ONE
I DIDN'T KNOW HOW
THINGS SHOULD BE
DONE,
BUT I CAN'T THINK
ABOUT ANYTHING
ELSE BUT WOULDN'T LIVE
WITHOUT ANY OF YOU,
WHEN I WAS FIVE
I HAD MANY FRIENDS
BUT I ONLY HAD
ONE FRIEND LIKE YOU,
NOW I'M GROWN
BUT I WANT TO GO
THIRTEEN YEARS BACK
WHEN I WAS ON
YOUR LAP.

8. EVERY NIGHT!!

EVERY NIGHT IN THE
MIDDLE OF THE NIGHT
A THING COMES IN MY
MIND,
WOULD THINGS BE
LIKE THEY ARE NOW
OR SOMETHING WILL
BE CHANGED,
THESE QUESTIONS ONLY
COME AT NIGHT AND
THE NEXT DAY
I FORGET,
WILL I BE CHANGED
WISH MY FRIENDS
WOULD ALWAYS BE
THE SAME,
AND EVERYTIME IN THE
MIDDELE OF THE NIGHT
THE SAME QUESTIONS COMES
IN MY MIND AND THEN I WRITE
IT DOWN, SO I'LL REMEMBER IT
NEXT TIME.

9. HIDE!

YOU DON'T HAVE TO
HIDE FROM ANYONE
ANYMORE,JUST FACE
THEM AND LET IT
GO,
DON'T LET PEOPLE SCARE
YOU OTHERWISE THEY WILL
ALWAYS BE BEHIND
YOU,
IF YOU HIDE FROM
ANYONE THAT MEANS YOU
ARE ASHAMED OF
SOMETHING YOU
DID,
JUST BE YOURSELF
NOT ONLY AROUND THE
PEOPLE YOU CARE BUT THE
PEOPLE YOU ARE
SCARED OF,
DON'T HIDE FROM PEOPLE
YOU CARE,THEY WILL NOT
DO ANYTHING YOU DON'T
LIKE,THEY WILL JUST KEEP

YOU AWAY FROM THE
PEOPLE YOU
DESPITE.

10. MY PRIDE

MY COUNTRY IS MY PRIDE
IT'S ALWAYS ON MY
SIDE ,EVEN WHEN
I'M WRONGOR
RIGHT,
IT'S THE LIFE OF OUR
NATION ,LOOK IT'S
SUCH A WONDERFUL
CREATION,
WE TRY OUR BEST
NOT TO FIGHT WITH THE
REST,BUT SOME PEOPLE
DON'T GET IT, IT'S NOT THAT
EASY TO BE THE
BEST,
WE ARE A DEMOCRACY
FULL OF HAPPINESS AND LOVE
BUT MY COUNTRY IS
ENOUGH FOR ME TO
GET THROUGH
EVERYTHING,
WHEN I SEE MY FLAG
I CRY WITH PRIDE

CAUSE MY NATION
IS MY LIFE.

11. LIKE A STRANGER!

YOU PLANTED A SEED
IN MY MIND,WHICH
IS GROWN NOW,
WHO IS TRYING HER
BEST TO BE
KIND,
YOU CAME IN MY
LIFE, LIKE A STRANGER
AND THEN BECAME
THE MOST IMPORTANT
PART OF MY
LIFE,
IT'S BEEN FEW
YEARS SINCE
I KNOW YOU,BUT
IT FEELS LIKE I KNEW
YOU FOR A
LONG TIME,
WHEN I WAS NOT
SURE I COULD DO IT
YOU TOLD ME,LIFE
IS FULL OF UPS AND
DOWNS,BUT YOU HAVE

TO BE SURE WHAT
SHOULDN'T GO
WRONG,
YOU'RE NOT JUST MY
TEACHER,YOU'RE LIKE
MY SECOND MOTHER,
WHO HELD MY HAND
WHEN I CROSS THE ROAD
AND ASK ME CALL
YOU WHEN I REACH HOME.

12. ON THE ROAD

I'M TRAVELING ON THE
ROAD WITH FRIENDS BY MY
SIDE,IT'S NEVER BEEN BETTER
CAUSE I WAS ALONE
EVERYTIME,
I CAN SEE GREEN DOWN
TOWN HILLS,THE BLUE SKY,WELL WHO
IS WITH ME ALMOST
EVERTIME,
THE VIRIDESCENT PLANTS NEVER
GET BORED OF SEEING THE
SAME THING ALL OVER
AGAIN,
I AM WITH MY FRIEND'S
BUT I AM BUSY ADMIRING
THE PLACE,
I CAN SEE THE UNIQUE DISTINCTIVE
PEOPLE ON THE WAY TO
HEAVEN I JUST WISH
I COULD STAY THERE
FOREVER.

13. STUCK AT ONE PLACE

I'M STUCK AT ONE PLACE
THERE IS NO WAY OUT,
I ENDEAVOURED TO
GET OUT,
IT'S REALLY DARK EVERYTIME
I OPEN MY EYES
I'M A LITTLE SCARED
HOW WILL I GET
OUT THIS TIME,
I KNOW I'LL BE OUT
AFTER A FEW DAYS
BUT IT FEELS LIKE
IT'S BEEN YEARS
SINCE I'VE
SEEN THIS
PLACE,
I HOPE I'LL BE BETTER
WHEN I'LL SEE THE
OUTSIDE-WORLD BUT
I JUST WANT TO FEEL
THE FREEDOM WHICH
I NEED,

I KNOW THIS IS NOT
FOR A LIFE TIME BUT
I AM WORRIED WHAT
IF IT LASTS FOREVER.

14. NOTHING IN MY MIND

NOTHING IS COMMING IN MY
MIND EXPT THE WORK
I HAVE TO DO ON
TIME,
I AM THINKING REALLY HARD
BUT CAN'T THINK OF ANYTHING
BUT WHAT I AM GOING
TO DO NEXT,
I AM PUTTING MYSELF IN
PRESSURE,WHAT TO DO
NOW CAUSE I CAN'T
SEE ANYTHING IN
FRONT OF ME,
ALL I CAN THINK OF IS,
I'M SITTING ON THE
CLOUDS,WHISPERING TO
THE BIRDS,AND SEEING
THE BRILLIANT BRIGHT
SUN,
I'LL TRY TO THINK OF SOMETHING
AGAIN,TOMORROW,BUT IF I
CAN'T,I'LL NOT FEEL

SORROW.

15. BELIVE

BELIVE IN EVERYTHING YOU SEE
IT MIGHT NOT BE REAL
BUT IT CAN BE,
THE THINGS YOU SEE AREN‘T
ALWAYS TRUE,UNLESS YOU
MAKE THE WORLD
BLOOM,
MONSTERS ARE REAL BUT
DRESSED LIKE PEOPLE
NOBODY CAN RECOGNISE
THEM EXCEPT YOU,
EVEN MERMAIDS ARE REAL
PEOPLE DON'T BELIVE ME
THEY LAUGH AT ME,BUT
THATS NOT AN EASY
THING TO TELL WHAT
YOU FEEL,
I CAN SEE THE FUTURE AND
ITS NOT VERY BRIGHT,CAUSE
PEOPLE DON'T BELIVE IN
ANYBODY WHEN THEY COME
OUT OF THERE OWN
SIGHT.

16. AN EVIL IS COMMING

IT COMES LIKE WATER
AND LEAVES LIKE A DAUGHTER
COMES BACK LIKE A
SLAUGHTER,
IT HAS NO END,IT MAKES
A FLOOD AND LEAVES EVERYONE AN
ORPHAN JUST FOR HIS FUN,
PEOPLE ARE ROAMING AROUND
MEETING PEOPLE WITH WHOM
THEY WANT TO HANG OUT,
IT HAS STOPPED BUT NOT
FOREVER IT WILL VANISH THE
WHOLE WORLD ,NO ONE WILL
BE ALIVE AFTER
SOMETIME,
THE SMILING FACES OF LITTLE
HAPPINESS WON'T LAST FOR
LONG CAUSE HE WILL BE
BACK AFTER DAWN.

17. A LADDER!

MY LIFE IS LIKE A LADDER
I THINK YOURS WOULD BE TOO,
IT'S ARDUOUS TO GO UP
BUT IT TAKES A SECOND TO
COME DOWN,
I WAS TALKING TO MYSELF
WHAT SHOULD I DO TO BE THE
ONE,WHAT SHOULD I BE LIKE TO
FEEL THE BEST PERSON,
I WAS TRYING TO FIGURE
EVERYTHING OUT ,SUDDENLY EVERYTHING
BECAME WRONG AT ONCE,I WASN'T ABLE TO
HANDLE IT
AND THEN IT GOT OUT OF HAND,
ALL THE HARD WORK I DID
ALL MY LIFE WAS GONE
BECAUSE OF ONE LITTLE
MISTAKE,
BUT THAT MISTAKE TAUGHT ME
SOMETHING VALUABLE,WHICH
I WON'T GET IT IF I WOULDN'T GO
THROUGH IT.

18. I'VE SEEN

I'VE SEEN YOUR BAD SIDE BUT
NOT YOUR GOOD ONE,IT WOULD
BE DIFFERENT FOR ONCE IF YOU I'M
CHANGED FOR SOMEONE,
I KNOW YOR PAST BUT NOT
YOUR FUTURE,IT'S NOT IN MY
HANDS BUT IF YOU LET ME
IN,I CAN TELL YOU WHAT
IT COULD BE,
I'M NOT SURE YOU'LL LIKE IT
BUT I'LL TRY TO GIVE YOU
BEST ADVICE SO YOU COULD
DO BETTER IN LIFE,
I'VE SEEN YOU ANGRY BUT NOT HAPPY
DON'T YOU HAVE ANY REASONS TO
BE CHEERFUL ANYMORE,
I'VE SEEN YOR BAD SIDE,BUT
NOT YOU'RE GOOD ONE, I HOPE
I'LL BE CAPABLE TO SEE THAT
SOMETIME.

19. THE TALES THAT TAUGHT ME

THE CROCDILE BETRYED THE
MONKEY,HE WAS SAD BUT
WHAT CAN HE DO EXCEPT
TO GET MAD,
NOW HE KNOWS WHOM TO
TRUST AND WHOM TO NOT
FROM NOW ONWARDS HE
WILL ACTUALLY REMEMBER
THIS THOUGHT,
THE LION WAS SO FOOLISH THAT
HE TRIED TO KILL HIMSELF WHO
WAS IN THE WELL,BUT THE
RABBIT WAS NOT,SO HE TRICKED
HIM AND HE LITALLY FELL
AFTER THAT IT WAS HIS
FAREWELL,
HE ATE EVERY ANIMAL ALIVE
IN THE FOREST ONE BY ONE,
HE DIDNT FELT BAD,THEN
WHY SHOULD WE? WHEN
HE DIED,
THE MONGOOSE PROTECTED THE

CHILD BUT IN RETURN HER
MOTHER KILLED HIM,THEN
CRIED,
FROM ALL THESE STORIES I
HAVE SEEN HOW THERE LIFE
MIGHT HAVE BEEN.

20. WHEN YOU MISS!

WHEN YOU MISS THE ONES WHO
AREN'T WITH YOU AT THE PRESENT
TIME,YOU LOOK AT THE PICTURES
AND SAY THOSE WERE THE TIMES,
YOU PROMISE WE'LL TALK EVERYDAY,
BUT THEN YOU FORGET AND SAY
"OH I'M SORRY I FORGOT BUT
FROM NEXT TIME I WILL NOT,
YOU SEE YOUR OLD SELF AND SAY
I WAS SUCH A CUTIE PIE,AND
THE OTHER ONE IS PRETTY AS THE
WHOLE SKY,
WHEN YOU FINALLY MEET THEM
YOU HUG THEM SO HARD THAT YOU'LL
NEVER EVER LEAVE THEM AGAIN,
BUT WHEN YOU ARE GOING BACK
YOU START TO CRY,
BUT THEN YOU TRY TO STOP
YOURSELF AND SAY I'LL MEET
YOU AGAIN SOMETIME.

21. IMAGINE

IMAGINE THE THINGS YOU SEE,
NOT IN REAL LIFE BUT IN YOUR
DREAM,
IT CAN BE AN EYE-OPENING DAY
IF YOU JUST IMAGINE THE
THINGS YOU SAY,
FOR SOMETIME IT CAN BE
AMAZING BUT SOME PEOPLE
FIND IT CRAZY IF YOU FIND
AMAZING,
WHEN YOU ARE ALL ALONE
TAKE IT AS A ADVANTAGE
TO BE CHEERFUL ON YOUR
OWN,
IF YOU IMAGINE GOD INFRONT
PF YU DON'T BE SCARED WHAT
TO SPEAK JUST SAY"THANK YOU
FOR EVERYTHING YOU'VE GIVEN ME.

22. DANCING WITH MY EYES CLOSED

DANCING WITH MY EYES CLOSED
DON'T KNOW WHERE MY MIND GOES,
I CAN'T SEE YOU NOW BUT CAN
FEEL YOU TOO,
I DON'T KNOW WHERE YOU ARE BUT
I KNOW IT NOW,I CAN'T SEE YOU
HERE NOW BUT CAN FEEL YOU'RE
CLOSE,
I CAN'T SEE ANYBODY BUT I CAN SEE
YOU THERE INFRONT OF ME,STANDING
QUITLY IN THE CORNER WAITING
FOR ME,
I'M STANDING HERE BUT YOU CAN'T
SEE ME NOW THAT I'M GONE BUT
I'M RIGHT HERE FOR YOU IF
YOU DROWN,
DANCING WITH MY EYES CLOSED
DON'T KNOW WHERE I MIGHT GO,
NOW WITHOUT YOU BY MY SIDE,
I'M FEELING LONELY TONIGHT.

23. LUCKLESS GIRL!

I KNEW A LUCKLESS GIRL
SHE WAS ALWAYS QUIETLY SITTING
ON THE LAST BENCH,WHO DIDN‘T
LIKE TO TWIRL,
I OFTEN TRIED TO TALK TO HER,
BUT SHE NEVER REPLIED,I
STILL WONDER WHY DIDN’T SHE
HAVE THE DREAMS TO FLY,
SHE LOVED TO READ BOOKS,
WAS ALWAYS IN HER OWN
WORLD,AND NEVER CARED
SHE LOOKS,
SHE DIDN'T BELIVE IN MIRACLES
UNTIL SHE REALLY SAW AN
ANGEL AND A DEVIL,
I USED TO ADMIRE HER,CAUSE
SHE HAD SOMETHING THAT I
NEVER SAW IN ANYBODY
EVER AGAIN.

24. STRONG

I'M STRONG I WON'T BEND
DOWN EVEN IF YOU SCARE
ME OR NOT CARE FOR ME,
I DON'T NEED YOUR SYMPATHY,
GO GIVE IT TO SOMEBODY ELSE
CAUSE I KNOW YOU'LL GIVE YOUR
EMPATHY TO SOMEONE WHO DOSEN'T
FEEL,
YOU DON'T KNOW WHAT IS LOVE
AND YOU'LL NEVER KNOW
UNTIL YOU SEE YOUR LOVED ONES
GROW,
YOU CAN BE TEN FEET TALL
BUT THAT DOESN'T MAKE
YOU STRONGMYOU SHOULD HAVE
CONFIDENCE AND BE DETERMINED
THAT'S ALL,
I'M STRONG I WON'T FALL
DOWN EVEN IF YOU PUSH
ME CAUSE I HAVE STRENGHT
THAT WILL KEEP ME ON.

25. WINTER

I'M SITTING ON THE DECK WITH
HOT COFFEE IN MY HAND CAUSE
WINTER IS ARRIVING ON THE LAND,
THE TEMPERATURE IS DOWN TO
12 DEGREES BUT IT STILL DOESN'T
MATTER IF I HAVE BONFIRE BESIDE ME,
IT'S REALLY COLD OUTSIDE,IT SEEMS
LIKE I'M GOING TO FREEZEIN THE
COLD BREEZE,
PEOPLE ARE HOLDING HANDS UNDER
THEIR GLOVES,FEELS LIKE IT'S
LOVE,
AT THE END OF THE DAY ON EVERY
WINTER NIGHT EVERY CHILD HOPES,
MY PARENTS WILL KISS ME GOOD
NIGHT.

26. FIGHTER

IF I WAS A FIGHTER
WOULD GOD GIVE ME FAITH
EACH AND EVERY DAY?,
I WOULD HAVE FOUGHT FOR MY
NATION NOT ONLY FOR FREEDOM
BUT FOR WISDOM,
I STILL HAVE A DESIRE
WITHIN ME WHO DOESN'T WANT
TO BE AT HOME,BECAUSE I WANT
TO BE KNOWN,
I HAVE THE AGNOY IN ME
WHO WANT TO DEFEAT THE
ENEMY WHO IS INFONT OF ME,
IF I WAS A FIGHTER MY PEOPLE
WOULD GIVE ME HOPE TO WAKE
UP EVERY MORNING TO FIGHT AGAIN
WITHOUT LOATHE.

27. SOUND OF SILENCE

YOU ATTRACT PEOPLE BY YOUR
UNIQUE STYLE THAT NO ONE KNOWS
NOT EVEN WHO LIVES ABOVE
THE SKY,
HOW YOU STILL QUITE BY SEEING
THE SCARIEST THINGS AROUND
THAT YOU NEVER THOUGHT OF,
I CAN HEAR THE SOUND OF SILENCE
WHEN I STAY QUIET FOR SOMETIME
BEFORE SLEEP,
I HAVE SEEN A FLOWER
BLOOM,CAUSE I WAS SILENT
WHEN I SAW THE NATURE'S
BROOM,
WHEN I'M SILENT IN THE ROOM
ALONE,I CAN HEAR THE VOICE
FROM SILENCE HOME.

28. LIKE YOU!

YOU ATTRACT PEOPLE BY YOUR
UNIQUE STYLE THAT NO ONE KNOWS
NOT EVEN WHO LIVES ABOVE
THE SKY,
HOW YOU STILL QUITE BY SEEING
THE SCARIEST THINGS AROUND
THAT YOU NEVER THOUGHT OF,
I CAN HEAR THE SOUND OF SILENCE
WHEN I STAY QUIET FOR SOMETIME
BEFORE SLEEP,
I HAVE SEEN A FLOWER
BLOOM,CAUSE I WAS SILENT
WHEN I SAW THE NATURE'S
BROOM,
WHEN I'M SILENT IN THE ROOM
ALONE,I CAN HEAR THE VOICE
FROM SILENCE HOME.

29. MY MYSTERY

I WAS AWAKE THE WHOLE
NIGHT,I DID'T COMPLAIN,
BECAUSE I HAD NO ONE
TO WHOM I COULD,
I STUDIED AND TRIED NOT
TO CRY CAUSE THERE WAS
NO ONE I COULD DEPEND ON,
BECAUSE THEY LIED,
MY EYES ARE RED,BUT I'M
STILL WRITING,BECAUSE
I DON'T HAVE A CHOICE,
BUT I WON'T STOP TILL
MY EYES WOULD BE BLEEDING,
MY HANDS AE TIRED BUT
I'M NOT SO I'LL KEEP DOING
TILL I FINISH WHAT I'M
TAUGHT,
EVERYTHING JUST ENDED I
DIDN'T THOUGHT IT WOULD,
AND NOW IT'S FINALLY TRUE
THAT I CAN MAKE MY
DREAMS COME TRUE.

30. BLUE EYES!

I WAS FALLING INTO YOUR
BLUE EYES,I NEVER THOUGHT
I WOULD,
YOU ASKED ME WHY I
GAZED YOUR EYES WHENEVER
YOU SAT BESIDE ME,
BUT YOU NEVER KNEW
YOUR EYES HYPNOTIZE ME
WHEN YOU LOOKED SILENTLY
AT ME,
YOU SEEM LIKE A DREAM
TO ME,BUT FOR HIM
YOU WERE JUST AN
ORDINARY GIRL,
EVERYBODY ADORED YOUR
AZURE OPTIC EXPECT YOU,CAUSE
YOU SAW THEM YOUR WHOLE
LIFE BUT ME TOO.

31. TURN A PAGE

TURN A PAGE AND SEE
WHAT YOU HAVE DONE TO
ME,
WHEN I AM WITH YOU I FEEL
ALIVE AND FREE,IN THE NIGHT
WHEN YOU COME AND SLEEP
BESIDE ME,
TURN A PAGE AND SEE
HOW FAR I HAVE COME
WITH YOU LOSING ME,
I AM INCOMPLETE IN SOME
OR OTHER WAY,BECAUSE YOU LEFT ME
BEHIND,THE OTHER DAY,
TURN A PAGE FOR THE LAST TIME
AND TAKE A PEEK AT ME,
BECAUSE WHEN I WAKE UP
I WISH YOU WERE THE FIRST THING
I SEE.

32. ACTIONS

YOUR ACTIONS DON'T AFFECT ME
IT AFFECTS THE WHOLE WORLD
WHOSE EMOTIONS YOU CAN'T
SEE,
WHEN YUR STANDING IN THE
DARK YOU CAN SEE WHAT
A BLIND ALWAYS FEEL,
YOU GET SCARED WHEN YOU
DON'T HAVE ANYONE TO TALK,
TO,BUT HAVE YOU EVER THOUGHT
ABOUT THOSE WHO HAVE LIVED ALONE
THERE WHOLE LIFE,
EVERY LITTLE THING YOU DO
EVERYDAY,MEANS EVERYTHING
TO THE PERSON YOU HAVE NEVER
SEEN,
A LOT OF PEOPLE CAN THINK
BUT ONLY FEW HAVE THE GUTS
TO SAY WHAT THEY MEAN.

33. CHANGES

THERE ARE SOME CHANGES IN
OUR LIVES,SOME BAD,SOME NICE
THAT NO ONE REALISE,
IT'S NOT JUST YOU,IT'S ME
IT'S US THAT YOU DIDN'T BELIVED
BUT IT DOSEN'T MATTER NOW
THAT YOU DON'T SEE ME,
YOU SAW ME TWICE
YOU WILL REALISE ,I'M NOT
FINE,I'M HURT,I'M SCARED
THAT YOU HAVE GONE AWAY,
YOU BROKE ME WHEN YOU
WENT AWAY,YOU SAW ME CRY
BUT YOU DIDN'T SAY A THING
CAUSE YOU DID'T REALISE.

34. HOPE

HOPE IS WHEN THEY WHAT
SOMETHING TO BE TRUE,IT'S THE
LAST THING YOU THINK WHEN YOU
DON'T HAVE A CLUE,
IT GIVES YOU A SECOND
CHANCE NOT TO REPEAT
THE MISTAKES YOU HAVE
DONE BEFORE,
WHEN EVERYONE YOU
WANTED BESIDE YOU ARE NOT
THERE,WHEN EVERYTHING YOU
THOUGHT IS REAL,BUT IT'S NOT,
WHEN YOUR WHOLE LIFE
IS GOING WRONG,IT TAKES
YOU TO THE RIGHT LANE,
THEY GIVE A HOPE TO GO
ON IN LIFE WHEN YOU HAVE
NO REASONTO BE ALIVE.

9 798885 556217

Printed by Libri Plureos GmbH in Hamburg,
Germany